My Bilingual Talking Dictionary

Portuguese & English

Mantra Lingua

First published in 2005 by Mantra Lingua
Global House, 303 Ballards Lane, London N12 8NP
www.mantralingua.com

This TalkingPEN edition 2015
Text copyright © 2005 Mantra Lingua
Illustrations copyright © 2005 Mantra Lingua
(except pages 4-9, 42-49 Illustrations copyright © 2005 Priscilla Lamont)
Audio copyright © 2009 Mantra Lingua

With thanks to the illustrators:
David Anstey, Dixie Bedford-Stockwell, Louise Daykin,
Alison Hopkins, Richard Johnson, Allan Jones,
Priscilla Lamont, Yokococo

All rights reserved

A CIP record for this book is available from the British Library

Hear each page of this talking book narrated with the TalkingPEN!
1) To get started touch the arrow button below with the TalkingPEN.
2) To hear the word in English touch the 'E' button at the top of the pages.
3) To hear the word spoken in an English sentence touch the 'S' button at the top of the pages.
4) To hear the language of your choice touch the 'L' button on the top of the pages.
5) Touch the square button below to hear more information about using the Dictionary with the TalkingPEN.

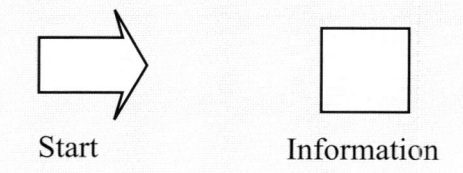

Start   Information

Contents

Eu
Myself — page 4-5

Roupas
Clothes — page 6-7

Família
Family — page 8

Casa
Home — page 9

Casa e recheio
House and Contents — page 10-11

Fruta
Fruit — page 12-13

Vegetais
Vegetables — page 14-15

Comida e bebida
Food and Drink — page 16-17

Hora da refeição
Meal Time — page 18-19

Cidade
Town — page 20-21

Rua principal
High Street — page 22-23

Segurança rodoviária
Road Safety — page 24-25

Transporte
Transport — page 26-27

Animais da quinta
Farm Animals — page 28-29

Animais selvagens
Wild Animals — page 30-31

Litoral
Seaside — page 32-33

Parque infantil
Playground — page 34-35

Sala de aula
Classroom — page 36-37

Mochila
School Bag — page 38-39

Computadores
Computers — page 40-41

Disfarces
Dressing Up — page 42-42

Brinquedos e jogos
Toys and Games — page 44-45

Desporto
Sport — page 46-47

Música
Music — page 48-49

Conteúdos

Espaço
Space — page 50-51

Tempo
Weather — page 52-53

Meses do ano
Months of the Year — page 54

Estações do ano
Seasons — page 54

Dias da semana
Days of the Week — page 55

Horas
Telling the Time — page 55

Cores
Colours — page 56

Formas
Shapes — page 56

Números 1-20
Numbers 1-20 — page 57

Opostos
Opposites — page 58-59

Índice
Index — page 60-64

Myself

olhos
ol-yoosh
eyes

cabelo
kah-beh-loo
hair

boca
baw-kah
mouth

orelhas
oh-rel-yash
ears

dentes
den-tesh
teeth

mão
maw
hand

polegar
poo-le-gah-r
thumb

pulso
pool-soo
wrist

dedos
day-doosh
fingers

cintura
sin-too-rah
waist

pés
pesh
feet

dedos dos pés
day-doosh doosh pesh
toes

feliz
fe-leesh
happy

triste
trish-te
sad

zangado
zan-gah-doo
angry

ciumento
sioo-men-too
jealous

entusiasmado
en-too-see-ash-ma-doo
excited

Eu

cara
ca-ra
face

cabeça
kah-beh-sah
head

nariz
na-ree-sh
nose

pescoço
pesh-caw-soo
neck

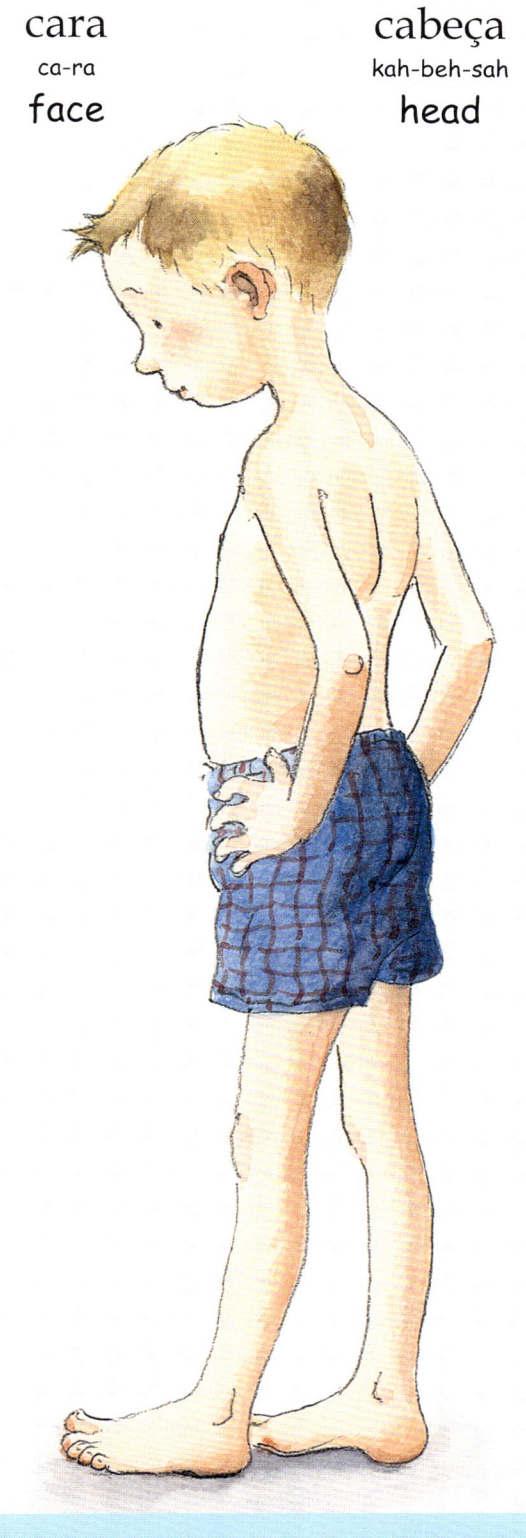

braço
bra-soo
arm

ombros
om-broosh
shoulders

estômago
esh-taw-ma-goo
stomach

cotovelo
coo-too-veh-loo
elbow

joelho
joo-el-yoo
knee

costas
cosh-tash
back

tornozelo
toor-noo-ze-loo
ankle

perna
per-nah
leg

doente
doo-en-te
sick

esfomeado
esh-faw-mee ah-doo
hungry

assustado
a-soosh-ta-doo
scared

tímido
tee-mee-doo
shy

cansado
can-sah-doo
tired

Clothes

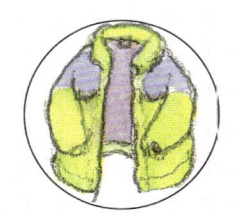

casaco
ca-zah-coo
coat

cachecol
cah-che-col
scarf

t-shirt
tee-shirt
t-shirt

vestido
vesh-tee-doo
dress

saia
sai-yah
skirt

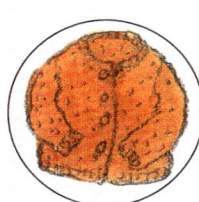

casaco de malha
ca-za-coo de mal-ya
cardigan

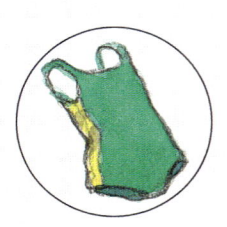

fato de banho
fah-too de ban-yoo
swimming costume

collants
caw-lansh
tights

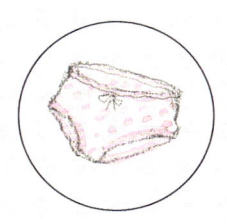

cuecas de senhora
coo-eh-cash de sen-yor-ah
knickers

sapatos
sa-pah-toosh
shoes

Roupas

luvas
loo-vash
gloves

chapéu
sha-pay-oo
hat

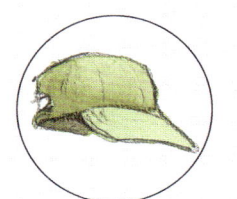

camisa
ca-mee-zah
shirt

blusão
bloo-zanw
jumper

calças
cal-sash
trousers

calções
cal-so-eesh
shorts

calções de banho
cal-so-eesh de ban-yoo
swimming trunks

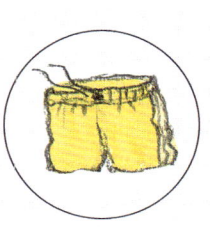

meias
mei-ash
socks

cuecas
coo-eh-cash
underpants

ténis
te-neesh
trainers

Family

Família

avó
ah-vo
grandmother

avô
ah-voh
grandfather

avô
ah-voh
grandfather

avó
ah-vo
grandmother

tia
tee-ah
aunt

pai
pah-ee
father

mãe
ma-ee
mother

tio
tee-oo
uncle

irmão
ir-ma-oo
brother

irmã
ir-man
sister

filho
feel-yoo
son

filha
feel-yah
daughter

bebé
beh-beh
baby

Home   Casa

telhado
tel-yah-doo
roof

sótão
soh-ta-oo
attic

janela
jah-neh-la
window

casa de banho
cah-sa de ban-yoo
bathroom

quarto
coo-ahr-too
bedroom

sala de jantar
sah-la de jan-tahr
dining room

cozinha
coo-zeen-ya
kitchen

hall de entrada
oh-le de en-tra-da
hallway

parede
pa-reh-de
wall

sala/sala de estar
sah-lah de esh-tar
lounge/living room

escada
esh-cah-da
staircase

porta
pohr-ta
door

9

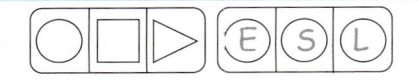

House and Contents

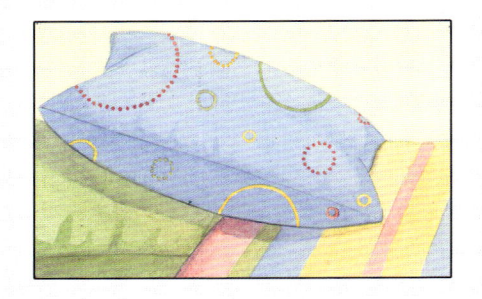

almofada
al-moo-fah-da
pillow

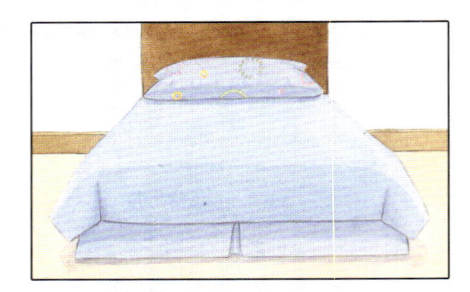

cama
ca-ma
bed

cobertor
coo-ber-towh
blanket

caixote do lixo
cai-show-te doo lee-shoo
bin

ventoinha
ven-too-in-ya
fan

candeeiro
can-dee-ei-roo
lamp

telefone
te-le-foh-ne
telephone

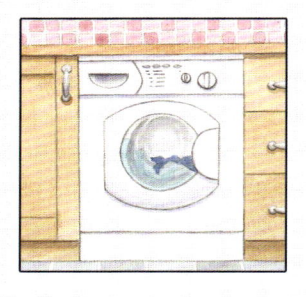

máquina de lavar roupa
mah-kee-na duh la-var row-pa
washing machine

torradeira
too-ra-dei-ra
toaster

chaleira
sha-lei-ra
kettle

torneira
toor-nei-ra
tap

frigorífico
free-goo-ree-fee-cuu
fridge

fogão
foo-gawn
cooker

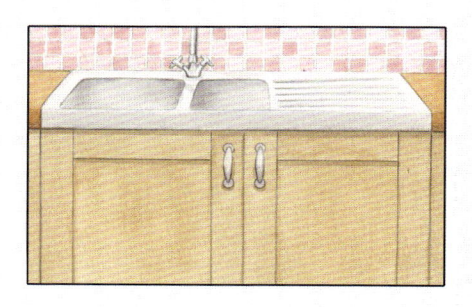

lava-louça
lah-va low-sa
sink

Casa e recheio

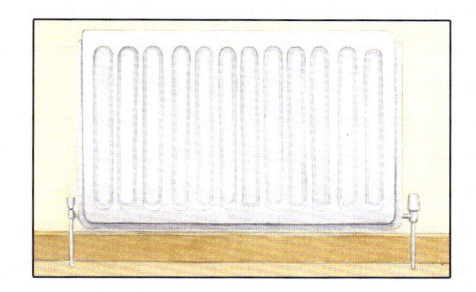

radiador
rah-dee-a-dor
radiator

banheira
ban-yei-ra
bath

toalha
too-al-ya
towel

espelho
esh-pel-yoo
mirror

sanita
sa-nee-ta
toilet

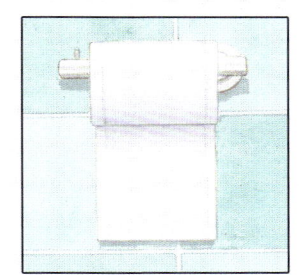

rolo de papel higiénico
roh-loo de pah-pewl ee-jee-eh-nee-coo
toilet roll

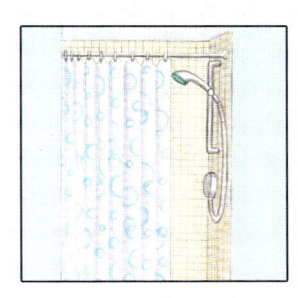

duche
doo-she
shower

televisão
te-le-vee-sawn
television

rádio
rah-dee-oo
radio

cortinas
coor-tee-nash
curtains

armário
ar-mah-ree-yoo
cupboard

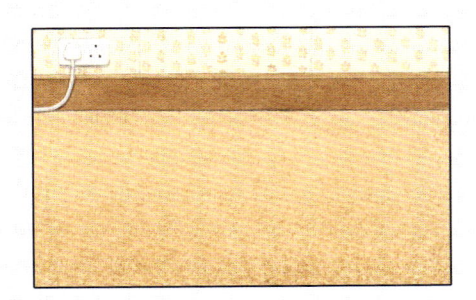

alcatifa
ahl-kat-eefa
carpet

sofá
soh-fah
sofa

mesa
may-sa
table

11

Fruit

banana
ba-na-na
banana

papaia
pa-pai-ya
papaya

pera
peh-ra
pear

melão
me-lawn
melon

ameixa
a-mei-sha
plum

limão
lee-mawn
lemon

cerejas
se-rei-zhash
cherries

morangos
moo-ran-goosh
strawberries

12

Fruta

uvas
oo-vash
grapes

ananás
a-na-nash
pineapple

manga
man-ga
mango

laranja
la-ran-zhah
orange

pêssego
pe-se-goo
peach

maçã
ma-san
apple

líchias
lee-shee-ash
lychees

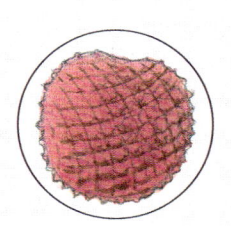

romã
roo-man
pomegranate

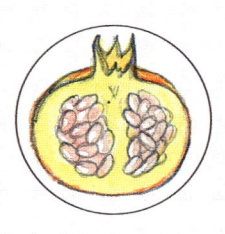

Vegetables

cebola
se-boh-la
onion

couve-flor
coh-ve flor
cauliflower

batata
ba-tah-tah
potato

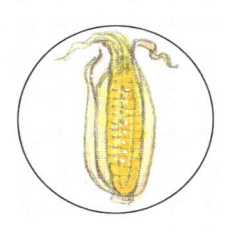

milho
meel-yoo
sweetcorn

cogumelo
coo-goo-meh-loo
mushroom

tomate
too-mah-te
tomato

feijões
fai-zhoynsh
beans

rabanete
ra-ba-neh-te
radish

14

Vegetais

alho
al-yoo
garlic

abóbora
a-boh-boo-ra
pumpkin/squash

pepino
peh-pee-noo
cucumber

brócolos
bro-coo-loosh
broccoli

pimento/pimentão
pee-men-too
pepper/capsicum

cenoura
se-noh-ra
carrot

alface
al-fah-se
lettuce

ervilhas
er-veel-yash
peas

15

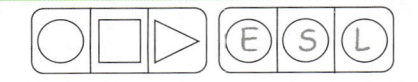

Food and Drink

pão
pown
bread

manteiga
man-tei-ga
butter

geleia
zhe-lai-ya
jam

sanduíche
san-doo-ee-sh
sandwich

açúcar
a-soo-cahr
sugar

mel
mehl
honey

cereais
se-re-aeesh
cereal

leite
lay-te
milk

massa chinesa
mah-sa shee-ne-za
noodles

arroz
a-rosh
rice

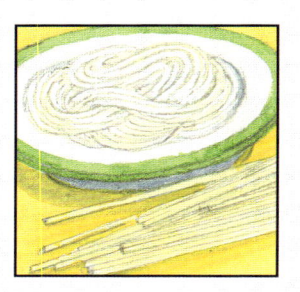

esparguete
esh-par-ge-te
spaghetti

pizza
pee-za
pizza

carne
car-ne
meat

peixe
paysh
fish

ovo
oh-voo
egg

queijo
kei-zhoo
cheese

16

Comida e bebida

chocolate shoo-coo-lah-te chocolate	**rebuçados** reh-boo-sa-doosh sweets	**bolo** bo-loo cake	**pudim** poo-deen pudding
iogurte ee-o-goor-te yoghurt	**gelado** zhe-lah-doo ice cream	**biscoito** beesh-coee-too biscuit	**batatas fritas de pacote** ba-tah-tahsh free-tahsh de pa-co-te crisps
batatas fritas ba-tah-tahsh free-tahsh chips	**ketchup** keh-choop ketchup	**mostarda** moosh-tar-da mustard	**sopa** so-pa soup
sumo de fruta soo-moo de froo-ta fruit juice	**água mineral** ah-goo-a mee-ne-ral mineral water	**sal** sahl salt	**pimenta** pee-men-ta pepper

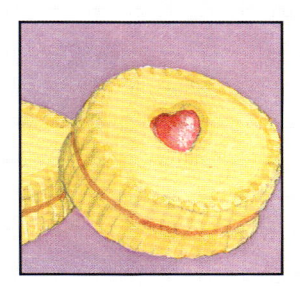

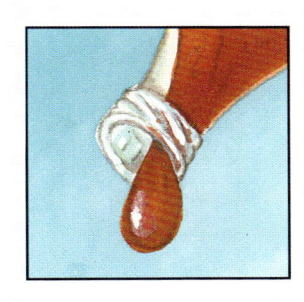

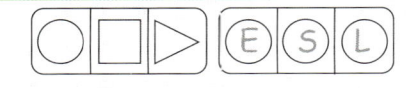

Meal Time

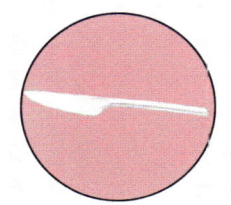

faca
fah-ca
knife

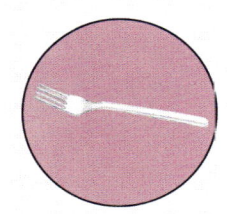

garfo
gahr-foo
fork

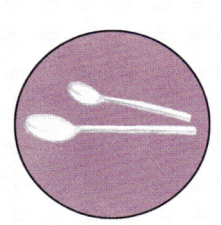

colher
cool-yer
spoon

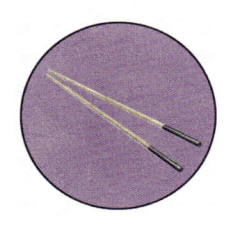

pauzinhos
pa-oo-zeen-yoosh
chopsticks

caneca
ca-neh-ca
mug

chávena
shah-ve-na
cup

copo
coh-poo
glass

Hora da refeição

prato
prah-too
plate

tigela
tee-jeh-la
bowl

caçarola
ca-sa-roh-la
saucepan

wok
oo-oh-ke
wok

frigideira
free-zhee-dei-ra
frying pan

termo
ter-moo
flask

lancheira
lan-shei-ra
lunchbox

19

Town

supermercado
soo-pehr-mer-cah-doo
supermarket

parque de estacionamento
pahr-ke de esh-ta-cee-oo-na-men-too
car park

centro desportivo
sen-troo desh-poor-tee-voo
sports centre

biblioteca
bee-blee-oo-te-ca
library

esquadra da polícia
esh-coo-a-dra da poo-lee-cee-a
police station

estação dos caminhos-de-ferro
esh-ta-sawn doosh ca-meen-yoosh de feh-roo
train station

quartel dos bombeiros
coo-ar-tel doosh bon-bei-roosh
fire station

20

Cidade

hospital
osh-pee-tal
hospital

parque
pahr-ke
park

cinema
see-ne-ma
cinema

garagem
ga-rah-zhen
garage

terminal de autocarros
ter-mee-nal de a-oo-to-cah-roos
bus station

lojas / armazéns
loh-zhash / ar-ma-zensh
shops/stores

escola
esh-coh-la
school

21

High Street

restaurante
resh-tau-ran-te
restaurant

florista
floo-rish-ta
florist

quiosque
kee-osh-ke
newspaper stand

livraria
lee-vra-ree-a
book shop

talho
tal-yoo
butcher

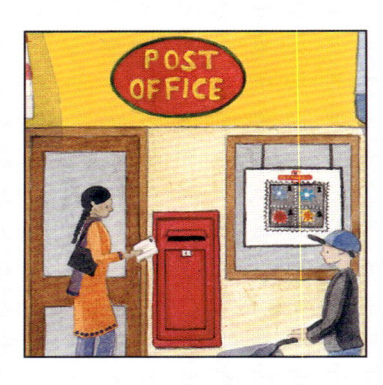

correios
coo-rei-oosh
post office

peixaria
pei-sha-ree-a
fishmonger

22

Rua principal

loja de frutas e legumes
loh-zhah de froo-tash ee le-gu-mesh
greengrocer

farmácia
far-mah-see-a
chemist

padaria
pah-da-ree-ah
bakery

banco
ban-coo
bank

loja de brinquedos
loh-zhah de brin-ke-doosh
toyshop

cafetaria
ca-fe-ta-ree-a
coffee shop

cabeleireiro
ca-be-lei-rei-roo
hairdressers

23

Road Safety

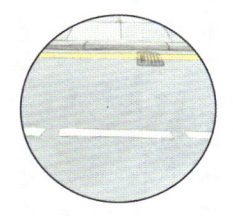

estrada
esh-tra-da
road

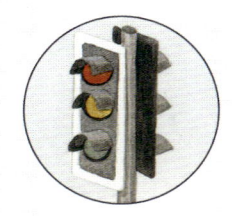

semáforo
se-mah-foo-roo
traffic light

luz vermelha
lush ver-mel-ya
red man

luz verde
lush vehr-de
green man

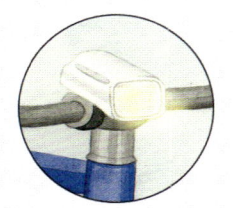

luzes
loo-zesh
lights

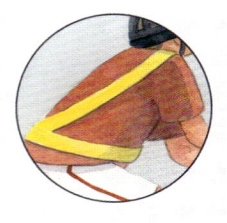

reflector
re-fle-c-tor
reflector

capacete de bicicleta
ca-pa-se-te de bee-cee-kle-ta
cycle helmet

passadeira de peõs
pa-sa-dei-ra de pee-oweesh
pedestrian crossing

24

Segurança rodoviária

andar
an-dahr
go

parar
pa-rahr
stop

olhar
ol-yar
look

escutar
eesh-coo-tahr
listen

travessia de crianças
tra-ve-see-a de kree-an-ssash
children crossing

oficial que ajuda a atravessar junto às escolas
ow-fe-thee-al ke ashuida a a-tra-ve-ssahr jootoo dash es-co-lash
school crossing patrol officer

cinto de segurança
sin-too de se-gu-ran-sa
seat belt

passeio
pa-sei-eeoo
pavement

25

Transport

avião
a-vee-awn
aeroplane

camião
cah-mee-awn
lorry/truck

carro
cah-roo
car

camioneta
ca-mee-oh-ne-ta
coach

barco
bahr-coo
boat

bicicleta
bee-cee-cle-ta
bicycle

comboio
con-boee-you
train

Transporte

motocicleta
mo-toh-see-cle-ta
motorbike

helicóptero
e-lee-co-pte-roo
helicopter

autocarro
aoo-to-ca-roo
bus

eléctrico
ew-leh-tree-coo
tram

caravana
ca-ra-va-na
caravan

navio
na-vee-oo
ship

riquexó
ri-ke-sho
rickshaw

Farm Animals

pássaro
pah-sa-roo
bird

cavalo
ca-vah-loo
horse

pato
pah-too
duck

gato
gah-too
cat

cabra
cah-brah
goat

coelho
coo-el-yoo
rabbit

raposa
ra-poh-za
fox

28

Animais da quinta

vaca
vah-ca
cow

cão
cawn
dog

ovelha
oh-vel-ya
sheep

rato
rah-too
mouse

galinha
ga-leen-ya
hen

burro
boo-ro
donkey

ganso
gan-soo
goose

Wild Animals

macaco
ma-cah-coo
monkey

elefante
e-le-fan-te
elephant

cobra
coh-bra
snake

zebra
ze-brah
zebra

leão
lee-awn
lion

hipopótamo
ee-poh-poh-ta-moo
hippopotamus

golfinho
gol-feen-yoo
dolphin

baleia
ba-lei-a
whale

Animais selvagens

panda
pan-da
panda bear

girafa
zhee-ra-fah
giraffe

camelo
ca-meh-loo
camel

tigre
tee-gre
tiger

urso
oor-soo
bear

pinguim
peen-goo-een
penguin

crocodilo
cro-coh-dee-loo
crocodile

tubarão
too-ba-rawn
shark

Seaside

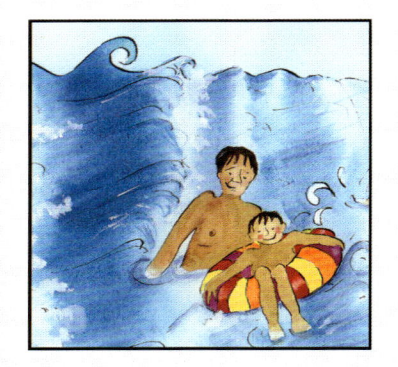

mar
mar
sea

ondas
on-dash
waves

praia
prai-ya
beach

salva-vidas
sal-va vee-dash
lifeguard

bronzeador
bron-ze-a-dor
sun lotion

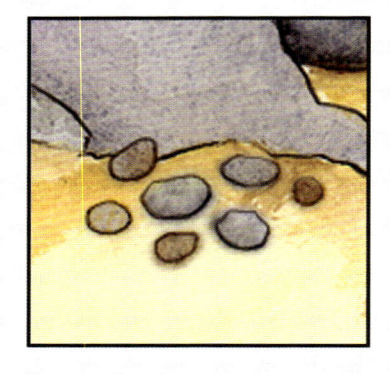

conchas
con-sha-sh
shells

seixos
sei-shoosh
pebbles

alga marítima
al-gah ma-ree-tee-ma
seaweed

32

Litoral

poça de água nas rochas
Poh-ssa dee ah-gooa nash row-shazs
rock pool

caranguejo
ca-ran-gay-zhoo
crab

estrela-do-mar
esh-tre-la doo mar
starfish

cadeira de praia
ca-dei-ra duh prai-ya
deckchair

areia
a-rei-ya
sand

castelo de areia
cash-te-loo de a-rei-ya
sandcastle

balde
bahl-de
bucket

pá
pah
spade

Playground

baloiço
ba-loy-soo
swing

carrossel
ca-roo-sel
roundabout

balancé
ba-lon-she
seesaw

caixa de areia
ca-ee-sha de a-rei-ya
sandpit

túnel
too-nel
tunnel

dentro
den-troo
in

fora
foh-ra
out

saltar
sahl-tahr
skip

34

Parque infantil

rede para trepar
re-depa-ra tre-pahrr
climbing frame

para cima
pa-ra si-ma
up

escorrega
esh-coo-re-ga
slide

para baixo
pa-ra baee-shoo
down

em cima
poor si-ma
over

debaixo
de-baee-shoo
under

à frente
ah fren-te
in front

atrás
a-trah-sh
behind

The Classroom

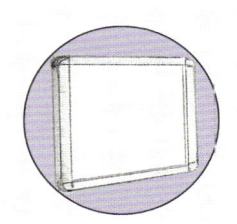

quadro branco
coo-ah-droo bran-coo
white board

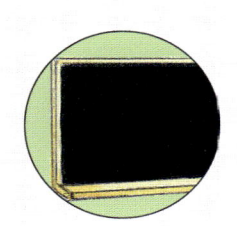

quadro negro
coo-ah-droo ne-groo
chalk board

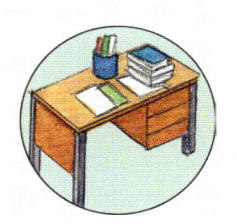

secretária
se-cre-tah-ree-ya
desk

cadeira
ca-dei-ra
chair

calendário
ca-len-dah-ree-yoo
calendar

gravador
gra-va-dor
tape recorder

cassete
ca-se-te
cassette tape

calculadora
cal-cu-la-doh-ra
calculator

Sala de aula

professor (m.)
professora (f.)
proo-fe-soh/proo-fe-soh-ra
teacher

livros
lee-vroosh
books

papel
pa-pel
paper

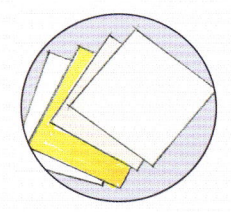

tinta
teen-ta
paint

pincel
peen-sel
paintbrush

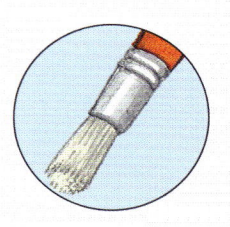

tesoura
te-soh-ra
scissors

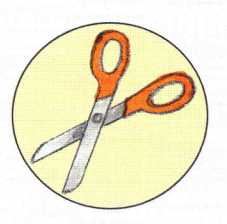

cola
coh-la
glue

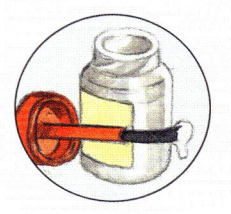

fita cola
fee-ta coh-la
sticky tape

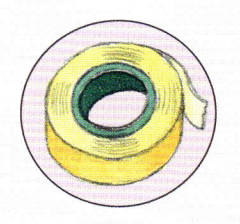

37

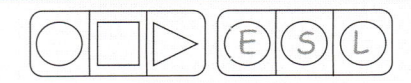

School Bag

caderno
ca-dehr-noo
writing book

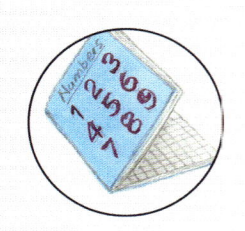

livro de matemática
lee-vroo de
ma-te-mah-tee-ca
maths book

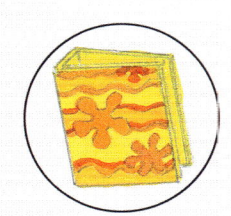

pasta
pash-ta
folder

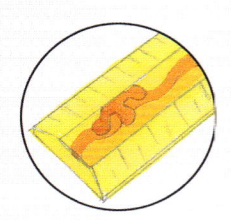

régua
reh-gwa
ruler

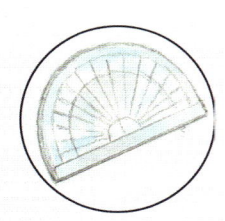

transferidor
transh-fe-ree-dor
protractor

lápis
lah-peesh
pencil

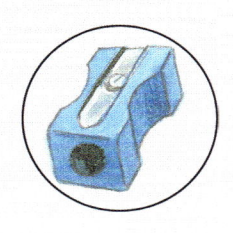

afia-lápis
a-fee-ya lah-peesh
pencil sharpener

38

Mochila

livro de leitura
lee-vroo de lei-too-ra
reading book

lápis de cera
lah-peesh de seh-ra
crayon

cordel
cur-dehl
string

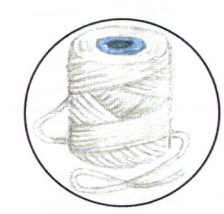

dinheiro
deen-yei-roo
money

compasso
com-pa-soo
compass

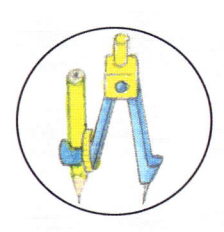

borracha
boo-ra-sha
rubber/eraser

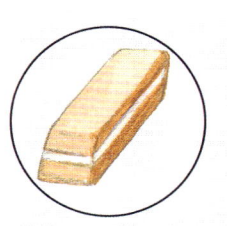

caneta de feltro
ca-ne-ta de fewl-troo
felt tip pen

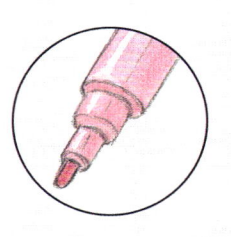

39

Computers

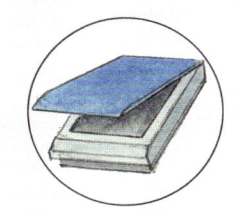

scanner
sca-ner
scanner

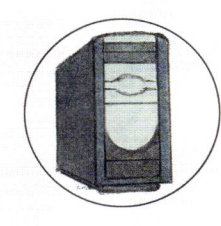

computador
com-poo-ta-dor
computer

monitor
moo-nee-tor
monitor

teclado
te-clah-doo
keyboard

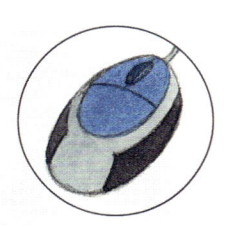

rato
rah-too
mouse

tapete para
o rato
ta-pe-te pa-ra rah-too
mouse mat

Computadores

impressora
im-pre-so-ra
printer

ecrã
eh-cran
screen

internet
in-ter-net
internet

correio electrónico
coo-rei-oo e-le-troh-nee-coo
email

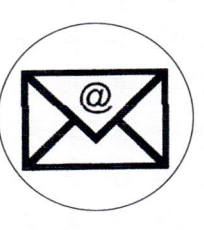

cd
say-day
cd disc

disquete
deesh-ke-te
floppy disc

Dressing Up

astronauta
ash-tro-naoo-ta
astronaut

polícia
poo-lee-cee-a
police person

veterinário
ve-te-ree-nah-ree-oo
vet

bombeiro
bom-bei-roo
firefighter

artista
ar-teesh-ta
artist

comerciante
Koo-mer-see-un-te
shop keeper

jóquei
zhoh-kei
jockey

cowboy
cow-boee
cowboy

cozinheiro
coo-zeen-yei-roo
chef

Disfarces

enfermeira
en-fer-mei-rah
nurse

mecânico
me-cah-nee-coo
mechanic

maquinista
mah-kee-neesh-ta
train driver

bailarina
baee-la-ree-na
ballet dancer

cantor
can-tor
pop star

palhaço
pal-yah-soo
clown

pirata
pee-rah-ta
pirate

feiticeiro
fei-tee-cei-roo
wizard

médico
meh-dee-coo
doctor

43

Toys and Games

balão
ba-lah-oo
balloon

contas
con-tash
beads

jogo de tabuleiro
zhoh-goosh de ta-boo-lei-roo
board game

boneca
boo-neh-ca
doll

casa de bonecas
ca-sah de boo-neh-cash
doll's house

papagaio de papel
pa-pa-gaee-oo de pa-pehl
kite

puzzle
pa-zle
puzzle

corda de saltar
cor-da de sahl-tahr
skipping rope

pião
pee-ah-oo
spinning top

44

Brinquedos e jogos

blocos de construção
blo-coosh de consh-troo-saw
building blocks

xadrez
sha-dresh
chess

dados
dah-doosh
dice

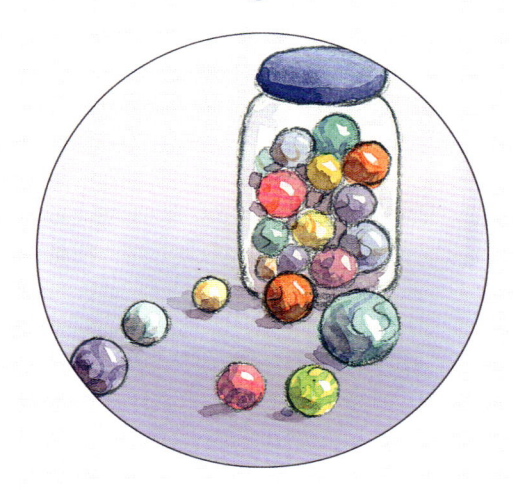

berlindes
ber-leen-desh
marbles

cartas de jogar
cahr-tash de joo-gahr
playing cards

fantoche
fan-tosh
puppet

ursinho de peluche
oor-seen-yoo de pel-oosh
teddy bear

pista de comboios
peesh-ta de com-boee-yoos
train set

carrinho
ca-reen-yoo
toy car

Sport

basquetebol
bash-ke-te-bohl
basketball

bola
boh-la
ball

críquete
cree-ke-te
cricket

badminton
bah-de-min-ton
badminton

natação
na-ta-sah-oo
swimming

patins
pa-tinsh
roller skates

raquete
rah-ke-te
racquet

patins para gelo
pa-tinsh pa-ra zheh-loo
ice skates

Desporto

ténis
teh-neesh
tennis

bastão
bash-tah-oo
bat

netball
nete-bal
netball

futebol
foo-te-bohl
football

ciclismo
see-clees-moo
cycling

râguebi
rahg-bee
rugby

prancha de skate
pran-sha de ska-te
skateboard

hóquei
o-kei
hockey

47

Music

bateria
ba-te-ree-ya
drum

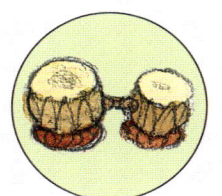

tabla
(tambores índios)
tah-bla (tam-bow-resh een-dee-ush)
tabla

clarinete
cla-ree-ne-te
clarinet

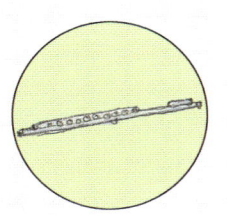

flauta
flah-oo-ta
flute

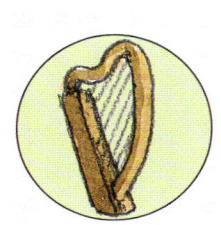

harpa
ar-pa
harp

teclado
teh-clah-doo
keyboard

guitarra
ghee-tah-ra
guitar

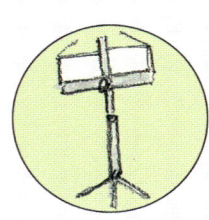

estante para pauta
esh-tan-te pah-ra pah-oo-ta
music stand

48

Música

triângulo
trian-goo-loo
musical triangle

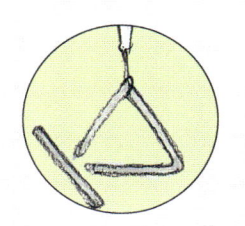

trompete
trom-peh-te
trumpet

maracas
ma-ra-cash
maracas

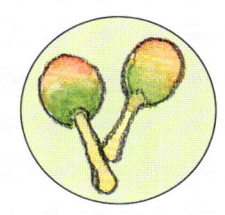

**gan gan
(tambor africano)**
gan-gan(tam-bor afri-ka-noo)
gan gan

piano
pee-a-noo
piano

flauta de bisel
flah-oo-ta de bee-sel
recorder

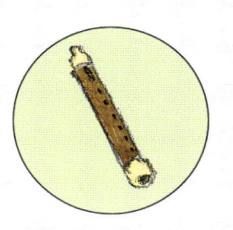

violino
vee-oo-lee-noo
violin

xilofone
shee-loh-foh-ne
xylophone

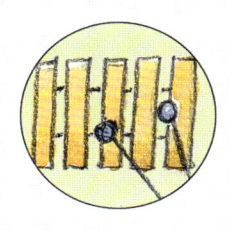

49

Space

Sol
sohl
sun

Mercúrio
mer-coo-ree-oo
Mercury

Vénus
veh-nush
Venus

Terra
teh-ra
Earth

Lua
loo-a
moon

nave espacial
nah-ve esh-pa-see-al
spaceship

estrela cadente
esh-tre-la ca-den-te
shooting star

foguetão
foo-ge-tah-oo
rocket

Espaço

Marte
mahr-te
Mars

Júpiter
zhoo-pee-ter
Jupiter

Saturno
sa-toor-noo
Saturn

Urano
oo-ra-noo
Uranus

cometa
coo-me-ta
comet

estrelas
esh-tre-lash
stars

Neptuno
neh-ptoo-noo
Neptune

Plutão
ploo-tah-oo
Pluto

51

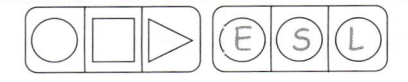

Weather

ensolarado
en-sol-a-ra-doo
sunny

arco íris
ar-coo ee-reesh
rainbow

chuvoso
shu-vo-soo
rainy

trovão
troo-vah-oo
thunder

relâmpago
re-lam-pa-goo
lightning

tempestuoso
tem-pesh-too-o-zoo
stormy

52

Tempo

ventoso
ven-toh-zoo
windy

nebuloso
ne-boo-low-zoo
foggy

nevoso
ne-voh-zoo
snowy

nublado
noo-blah-doo
cloudy

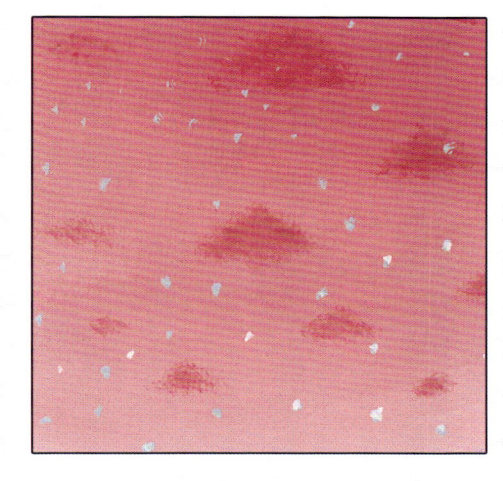

granizo
gra-nee-zoo
hail

gelado
zhe-lah-doo
icy

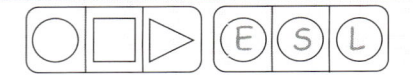

Months of the Year

Meses do ano

janeiro
ja-nei-roo
January

fevereiro
fe-ve-rei-roo
February

março
mahr-soo
March

abril
a-breel
April

maio
mah-ee-yoo
May

junho
zhoon-yoo
June

julho
zhool-yoo
July

agosto
a-gosh-too
August

setembro
se-tem-broo
September

outubro
ow-too-broo
October

novembro
noo-vem-broo
November

dezembro
de-zem-broo
December

Seasons

Estações do Ano

primavera
pree-ma-veh-ra
Spring

verão
ve-rah-oo
Summer

outono
ow-tow-noo
Autumn/Fall

inverno
in-vehr-noo
Winter

monção
mon-sah-oo
Monsoon

Days of the Week

Dias da semana

segunda-feira
se-goon-da fei-rah
Monday

terça-feira
ter-sa fei-rah
Tuesday

quarta-feira
koo-ar-ta fei-rah
Wednesday

quinta-feira
keen-ta fei-rah
Thursday

sexta-feira
seish-ta fei-rah
Friday

sábado
sah-ba-doo
Saturday

domingo
doo-min-goo
Sunday

Telling the Time

Horas

relógio
re-loh-zhee-oo
clock

dia
deea
day

noite
noy-te
night

manhã
man-yah
morning

fim do dia
feen doo deea
evening

relógio de pulso
re-loh-zhee-oo de pool-soo
watch

e um quarto
ee oom koo-ar-too
quarter past

e meia
ee mei-a
half past

um quarto para
uoom koo-ar-too pah-ra
quarter to

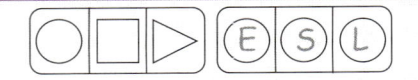

Colours　　　　　　　　　　　　　　　　　　Cores

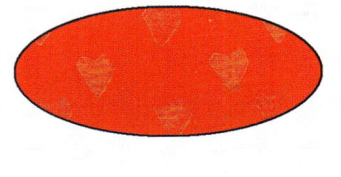

vermelho
ver-mel-yoo
red

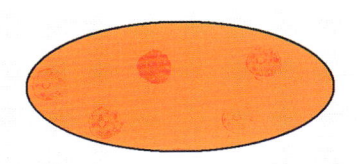

laranja
la-ran-zha
orange

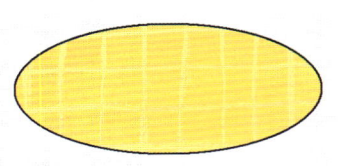

amarelo
a-ma-reh-loo
yellow

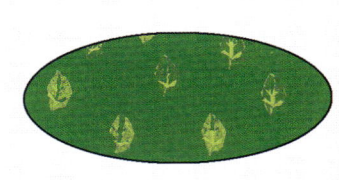

verde
ver-de
green

preto
pre-too
black

branco
bran-coo
white

cinzento
sin-zen-too
grey

azul
a-zool
blue

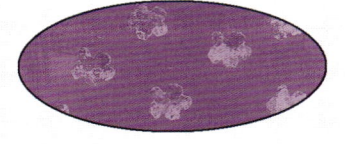

roxo
roh-shoo
purple

rosa
roh-za
pink

castanho
cash-tan-yoo
brown

Shapes　　　　　　　　　　　　　　　　　　Formas

círculo
seehr-coo-loo
circle

estrela
esh-tre-la
star

triângulo
tree-an-goo-loo
triangle

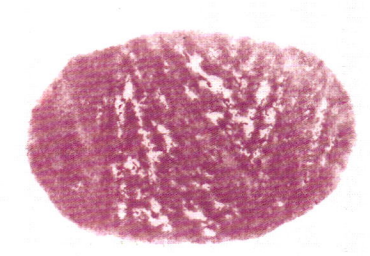

oval
oh-val
oval

cone
koh-ne
cone

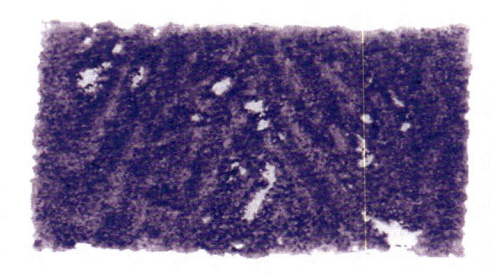

rectângulo
re-tan-goo-loo
rectangle

quadrado
kooa-drah-doo
square

Numbers 1-20   Números 1-20

	1	um oom **one**		11	onze on-ze **eleven**
	2	dois doeesh **two**		12	doze doh-ze **twelve**
	3	três tresh **three**		13	treze trey-ze **thirteen**
	4	quatro kooatroo **four**		14	catorze ka-tor-ze **fourteen**
	5	cinco seencoo **five**		15	quinze kin-ze **fifteen**
	6	seis seish **six**		16	dezasseis de-za-seish **sixteen**
	7	sete seh-te **seven**		17	dezassete de-za-seh-te **seventeen**
	8	oito oee-too **eight**		18	dezoito de-zoee-too **eighteen**
	9	nove noh-ve **nine**		19	dezanove de-za-no-ve **nineteen**
	10	dez desh **ten**		20	vinte veen-te **twenty**

Opposites

rápido
rah-pee-doo
fast

lento
len-too
slow

aberto
a-behr-too
open

fechado
fe-shah-doo
closed

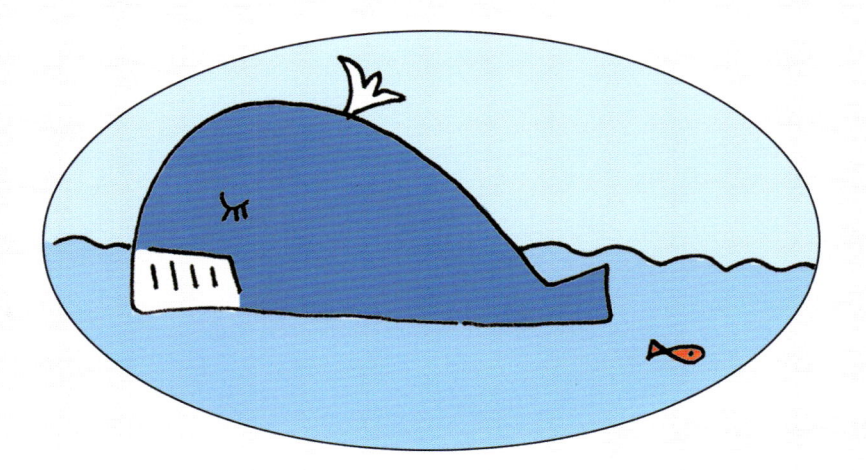

grande
gran-de
large

pequeno
pe-ke-noo
small

molhado
mool-ya-doo
wet

seco
seh-coo
dry

quente
ken-te
hot

frio
free-yoo
cold

doce
doh-se
sweet

azedo
a-ze-doo
sour

58

Opostos

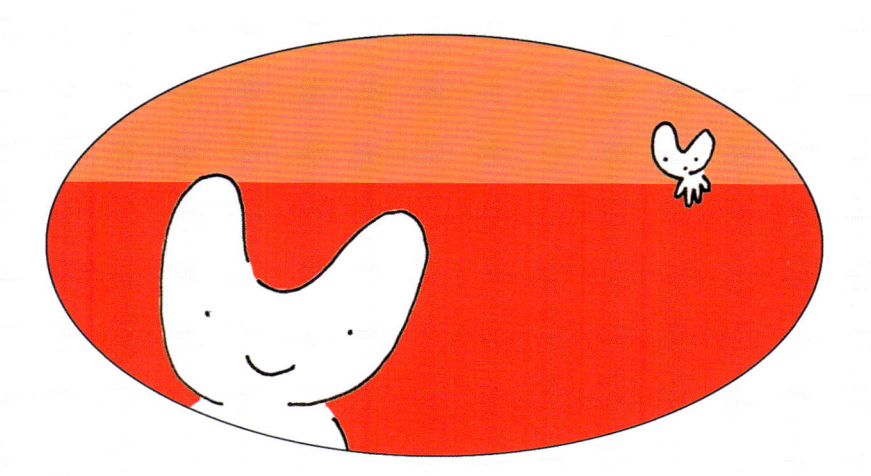

perto
pehr-too
near

longe
lon-zhe
far

esquerda
esh-ker-da
left

direita
dee-rei-ta
right

à frente
a-fren-te
front

atrás
a-trash
back

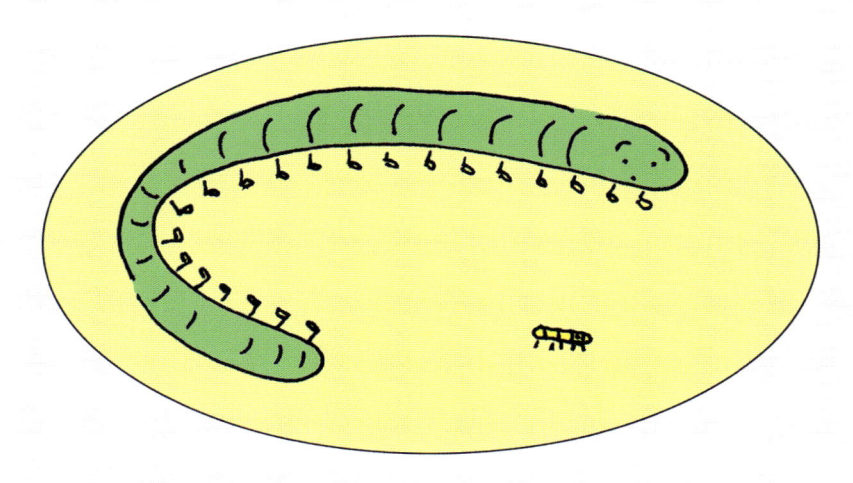

comprido
com-pree-doo
long

curto
koor-too
short

pesado
pe-sah-doo
heavy

leve
leh-ve
light

vazio
va-zee-oo
empty

cheio
shei-yoo
full

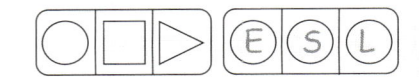

Index

Search for a word by picture or by the English word

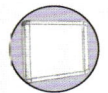

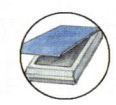

Classroom Page 36-37	teacher	socks	pink	printer	car mechanic	**Family** Page 8
books	white board	swimming costume	purple	scanner	chef	aunt
calculator	**Clothes** Page 6-7	swimming trunks	red	screen	clown	baby
calendar	cardigan	t-shirt	white	**Days of the Week** Page 55	cowboy	brother
cassette/tape	coat	tights	yellow	Monday	doctor	daughter
chair	dress	trainers	**Computers** Page 40-41	Tuesday	firefighter	father
chalk board	gloves	trousers	cd disc	Wednesday	jockey	grandfather
desk	hat	underpants	computer	Thursday	nurse	grandmother
glue	jumper	**Colours** Page 56	email	Friday	pirate	mother
paint	knickers	black	floppy disc	Saturday	police person	sister
paintbrush	scarf	blue	internet	Sunday	pop star	son
paper	shirt	brown	keyboard	**Dressing Up** Page 42-43	shop keeper	uncle
scissors	shoes	green	monitor	artist	train driver	**Farm Animals** Page 28-29
sticky tape	shorts	grey	mouse	astronaut	vet	bird
tape recorder	skirt	orange	mouse mat	ballet dancer	wizard	cat

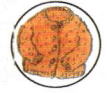

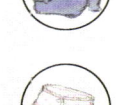

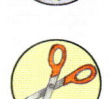

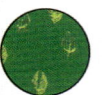

60

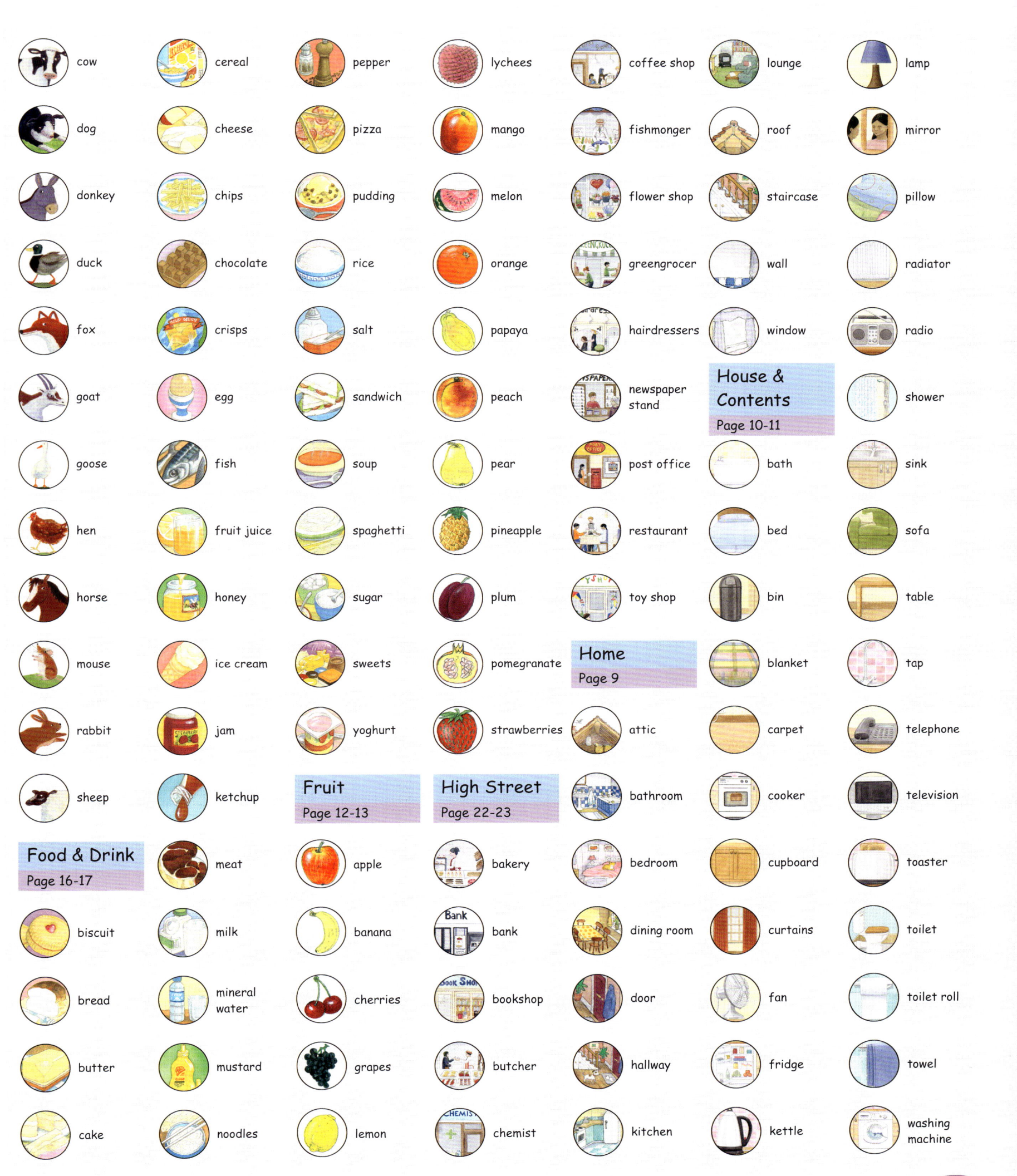

cow	cereal	pepper	lychees	coffee shop	lounge	lamp
dog	cheese	pizza	mango	fishmonger	roof	mirror
donkey	chips	pudding	melon	flower shop	staircase	pillow
duck	chocolate	rice	orange	greengrocer	wall	radiator
fox	crisps	salt	papaya	hairdressers	window	radio
goat	egg	sandwich	peach	newspaper stand	**House & Contents** Page 10-11	shower
goose	fish	soup	pear	post office	bath	sink
hen	fruit juice	spaghetti	pineapple	restaurant	bed	sofa
horse	honey	sugar	plum	toy shop	bin	table
mouse	ice cream	sweets	pomegranate	**Home** Page 9	blanket	tap
rabbit	jam	yoghurt	strawberries	attic	carpet	telephone
sheep	ketchup	**Fruit** Page 12-13	**High Street** Page 22-23	bathroom	cooker	television
Food & Drink Page 16-17	meat	apple	bakery	bedroom	cupboard	toaster
biscuit	milk	banana	bank	dining room	curtains	toilet
bread	mineral water	cherries	bookshop	door	fan	toilet roll
butter	mustard	grapes	butcher	hallway	fridge	towel
cake	noodles	lemon	chemist	kitchen	kettle	washing machine

61

Meal Time
Page 18-19

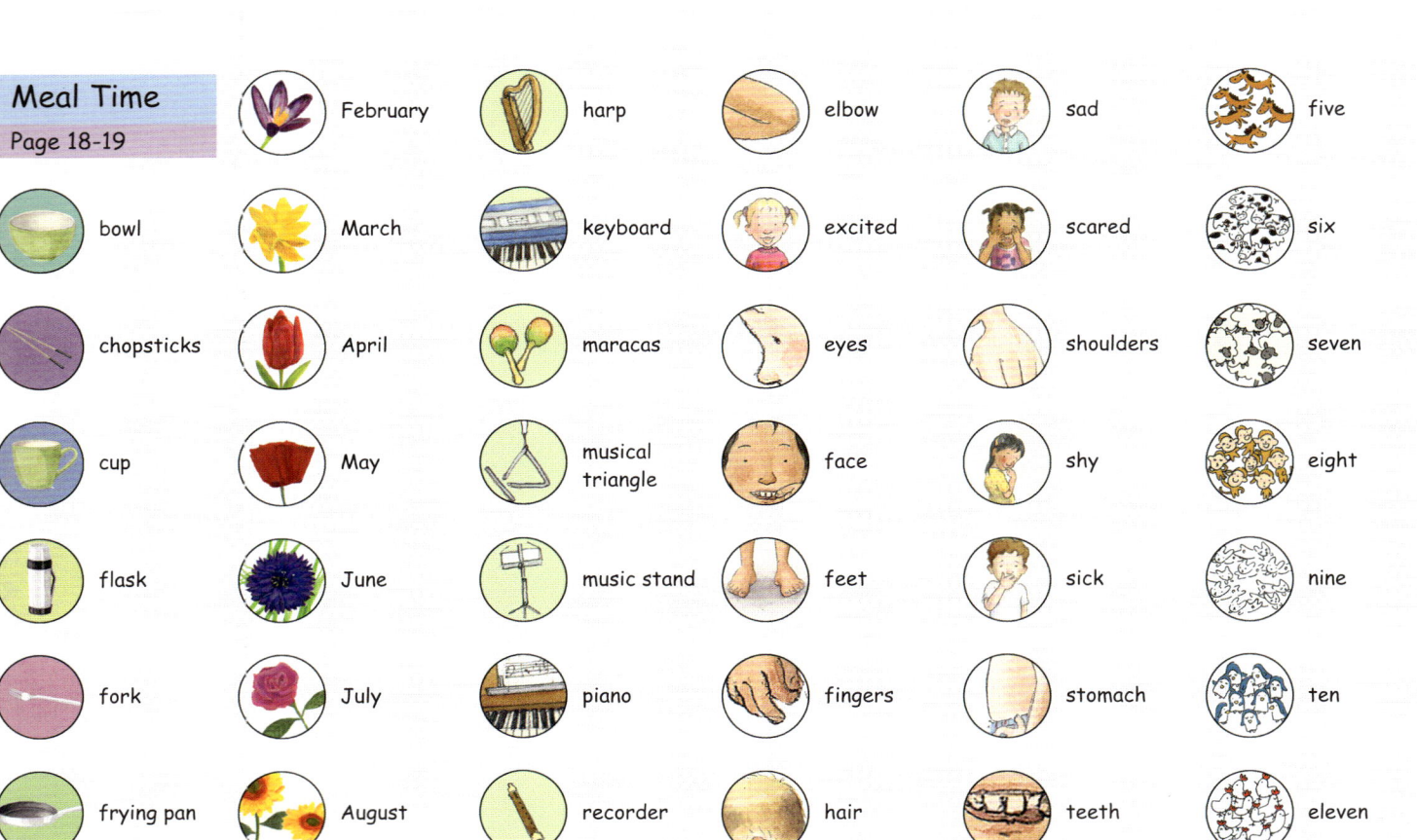

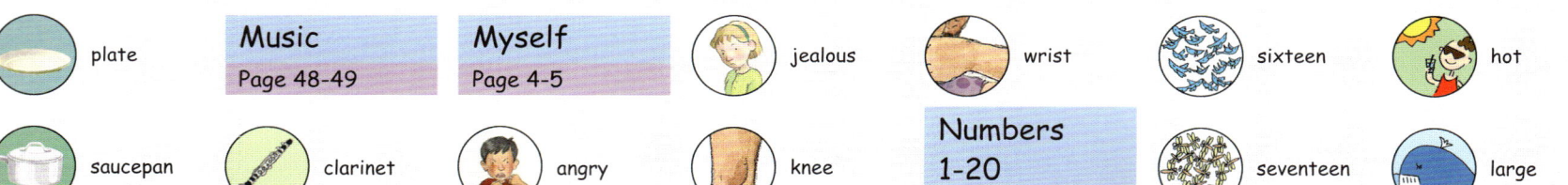

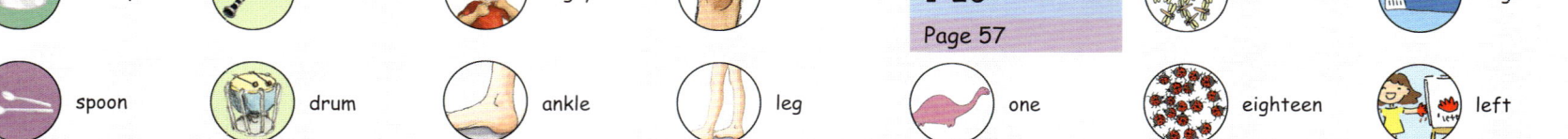

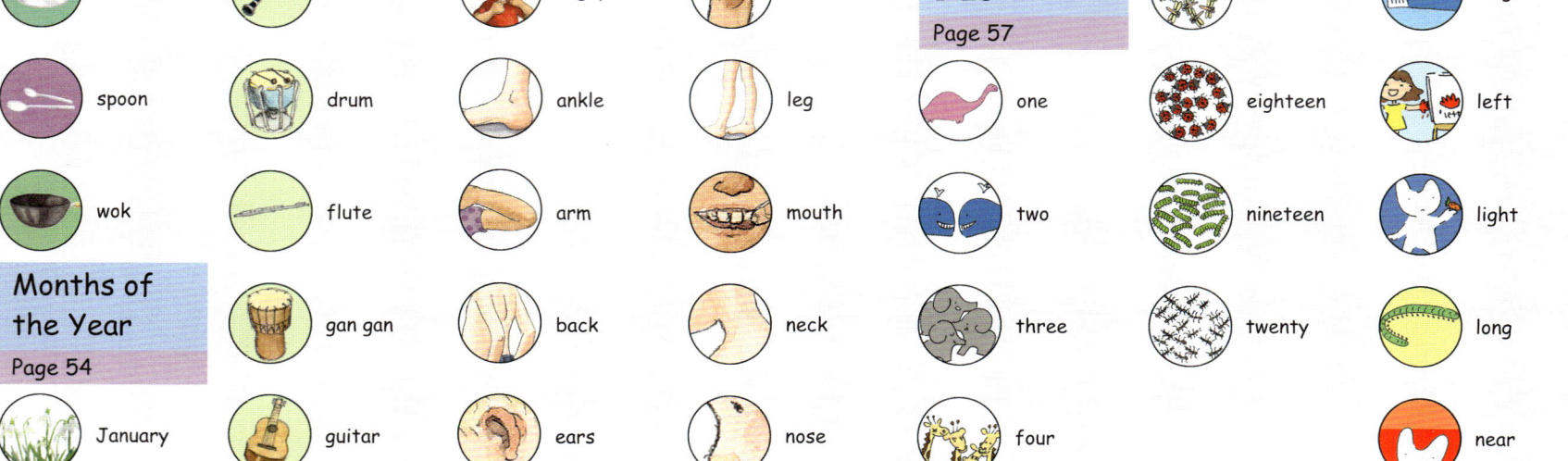

- bowl
- chopsticks
- cup
- flask
- fork
- frying pan
- glass
- knife
- lunchbox
- mug
- plate
- saucepan
- spoon
- wok

Months of the Year
Page 54

- January
- February
- March
- April
- May
- June
- July
- August
- September
- October
- November
- December

Music
Page 48-49

- clarinet
- drum
- flute
- gan gan
- guitar
- harp
- keyboard
- maracas
- musical triangle
- music stand
- piano
- recorder
- tabla
- trumpet
- violin
- xylophone

Myself
Page 4-5

- angry
- ankle
- arm
- back
- ears
- elbow
- excited
- eyes
- face
- feet
- fingers
- hair
- hand
- happy
- head
- hungry
- jealous
- knee
- leg
- mouth
- neck
- nose
- sad
- scared
- shoulders
- shy
- sick
- stomach
- teeth
- thumb
- tired
- toes
- waist
- wrist

Numbers 1-20
Page 57

- one
- two
- three
- four
- five
- six
- seven
- eight
- nine
- ten
- eleven
- twelve
- thirteen
- fourteen
- fifteen
- sixteen
- seventeen
- eighteen
- nineteen
- twenty

Opposites
Page 58-59

- back
- closed
- cold
- dry
- empty
- far
- fast
- front
- full
- heavy
- hot
- large
- left
- light
- long
- near

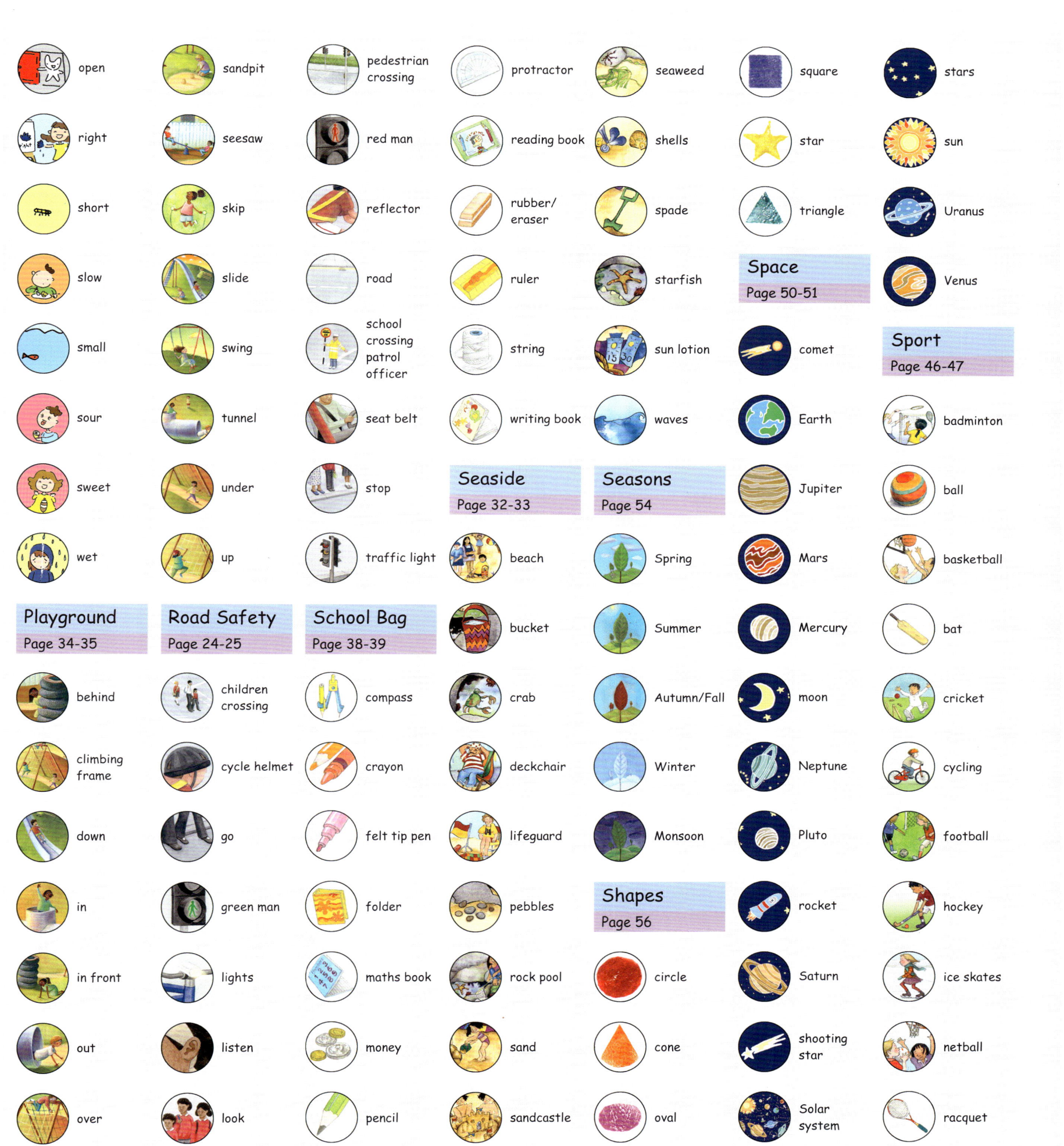

open	sandpit	pedestrian crossing	protractor	seaweed	square	stars	
right	seesaw	red man	reading book	shells	star	sun	
short	skip	reflector	rubber/eraser	spade	triangle	Uranus	
slow	slide	road	ruler	starfish	**Space** Page 50-51	Venus	
small	swing	school crossing patrol officer	string	sun lotion	comet	**Sport** Page 46-47	
sour	tunnel	seat belt	writing book	waves	Earth	badminton	
sweet	under	stop	**Seaside** Page 32-33	**Seasons** Page 54	Jupiter	ball	
wet	up	traffic light	beach	Spring	Mars	basketball	
Playground Page 34-35	**Road Safety** Page 24-25	**School Bag** Page 38-39	bucket	Summer	Mercury	bat	
behind	children crossing	compass	crab	Autumn/Fall	moon	cricket	
climbing frame	cycle helmet	crayon	deckchair	Winter	Neptune	cycling	
down	go	felt tip pen	lifeguard	Monsoon	Pluto	football	
in	green man	folder	pebbles	**Shapes** Page 56	rocket	hockey	
in front	lights	maths book	rock pool	circle	Saturn	ice skates	
out	listen	money	sand	cone	shooting star	netball	
over	look	pencil	sandcastle	oval	Solar system	racquet	
roundabout	pavement	pencil sharpener	sea	rectangle	spaceship	roller skates	

63

rugby	cinema	chess	boat	cucumber	foggy	crocodile	
skateboard	fire station	dice	bus	garlic	hail	dolphin	
swimming	garage	doll	car	lettuce	icy	elephant	
tennis	hospital	doll's house	caravan	mushroom	lightning	giraffe	

Telling the Time Page 55

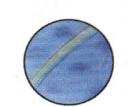

	library	kite	coach	onion	rainbow	hippopotamus	
clock	park	marbles	helicopter	peas	rainy	lion	
day	police station	playing cards	lorry/truck	pepper/capsicum	snowy	monkey	
evening	school	puppet	motorbike	potato	stormy	panda bear	
half past	shops/stores	puzzle	rickshaw	pumpkin/squash	sunny	penguin	
morning	sports centre	skipping rope	ship	radish	thunder	shark	
night	supermarket	spinning top	train	sweetcorn	windy	snake	
quarter past	train station	teddy bear	tram	tomato		tiger	

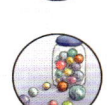

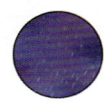

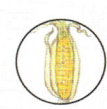

Wild Animals Page 30-31

quarter to		train set			bear	whale	

Toys and Games Page 44-45
Vegetables Page 14-15
Weather Page 52-53

watch	balloon	toy car	beans	cloudy	camel	zebra	
	beads		broccoli				

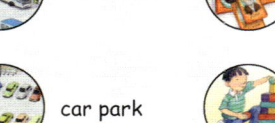

Town Page 20-21
Transport Page 26-27

bus station	board game	aeroplane	carrot	
car park	building blocks	bicycle	cauliflower	

64